WEDDING MUSIC
FOR CLASSICAL PLAYERS

To access companion recorded piano accompaniments online, visit:
www.halleonard.com/mylibrary

Enter Code
2548-4267-8000-6159

ISBN: 978-1-5400-2043-7

HAL•LEONARD®

Visit Hal Leonard Online at
www.halleonard.com

Contact Us:
Hal Leonard
7777 West Bluemound Road
Milwaukee, WI 53213
Email: info@halleonard.com

In Europe contact:
Hal Leonard Europe Limited
42 Wigmore Street
Marylebone, London, W1U 2RN
Email: info@halleonardeurope.com

In Australia contact:
Hal Leonard Australia Pty. Ltd.
4 Lentara Court
Cheltenham, Victoria, 3192 Australia
Email: info@halleonard.com.au

Depending on the situation, sometimes wedding service music must be abbreviated or expanded.
Feel free to find optional cuts, endings, or repeated sections as needed.

CONTENTS

JOHANN SEBASTIAN BACH
4 Air from Orchestral Suite No. 3[2]

6 Arioso (Sinfonia)[3]

8 Jesu, joy of man's desiring[3]

LUIGI BOCCHERINI
12 Minuet[2]

JEREMIAH CLARKE
16 The Prince of Denmark's March[3]

CHARLES GOUNOD
20 Ave Maria, adapted from Prelude in C Major by J.S. Bach[1]

GEORGE FRIDERIC HANDEL
24 Hornpipe from *Water Music*[2]

28 Largo from *Serse*[3]

GUSTAV HOLST
30 Jupiter Chorale from *The Planets*[3]

FELIX MENDELSSOHN
32 Wedding March from *A Midsummer Night's Dream*[3]

JEAN-JOSEPH MOURET
36 Rondeau[3]

JOHANN PACHELBEL
43 Canon[2]

HENRY PURCELL
46 Trumpet Tune[3]

ERIK SATIE
48 Gymnopédie No. 1[3]

FRANZ SCHUBERT
50 Ave Maria[2]

GOTTFRIED HEINRICH STÖLZEL
54 Bist du bei mir[3]

RICHARD WAGNER
40 Bridal Chorus from *Lohengrin*[2]

Pianists on the recordings: [1]Bill Casey, [2]Brendan Fox, [3]Richard Walters

The price of this publication includes access to companion recorded piano accompaniments online, for download or streaming, using the unique code found on the title page. Visit www.halleonard.com/mylibrary and enter the access code.

Air

from Orchestral Suite No. 3 in D Major, BWV 1068

Johann Sebastian Bach
Transcribed by Celeste Avery

13
16
19
22
rit.
tr
rit.

Arioso
(Sinfonia)
from Cantata, BWV 156

Johann Sebastian Bach
Transcribed by Celeste Avery

10
13
16
19
rit.
rit.

Jesu, joy of man's desiring

from Cantata, BWV 147

Johann Sebastian Bach
Transcribed by Celeste Avery

9
mf
12
p
mf
15
mp
18

* fermata for optional ending only

33
dim.
(,)
dim.
36
poco rit.
a tempo
f
poco rit.
f a tempo
39
42
rit.
rit.

Minuet

from String Quintet in E Major, Op. 11, No. 5

Luigi Boccherini
Transcribed by Celeste Avery

Con un poco di moto

14
cresc.
pp
18
1.
tr
mp
2. optional ending
22
Trio
mf
f
27
p
1.
2.
f
mp

32
mp
36
pp
mp
40
mf
mf
f
44
p
(,)
1.
2.
f
f
p

49
pp
cresc.
53
mf
mf
57
mp
61
pp
cresc.
65
rit.
rit.

The Prince of Denmark's March

Jeremiah Clarke
Transcribed by Celeste Avery

13
tr
16
f
f
tr
19
tr
22
tr
optional ending

25
mf
28
31
f
f
34

37
mf
mf
40
tr
f
f
43
tr
46
rit.
tr
rit.

Ave Maria

adapted from Prelude in C Major, BWV 846 by Johann Sebastian Bach

Charles Gounod
Transcribed by Celeste Avery

Andante con moto

11
cresc.
pp
cresc.
14
dim.
cresc.
17
p
cresc.
p
20
cresc.

22
dim.
p
25
cresc. molto
cresc. molto
f
28
p
pp
30
cresc. molto
cresc. molto

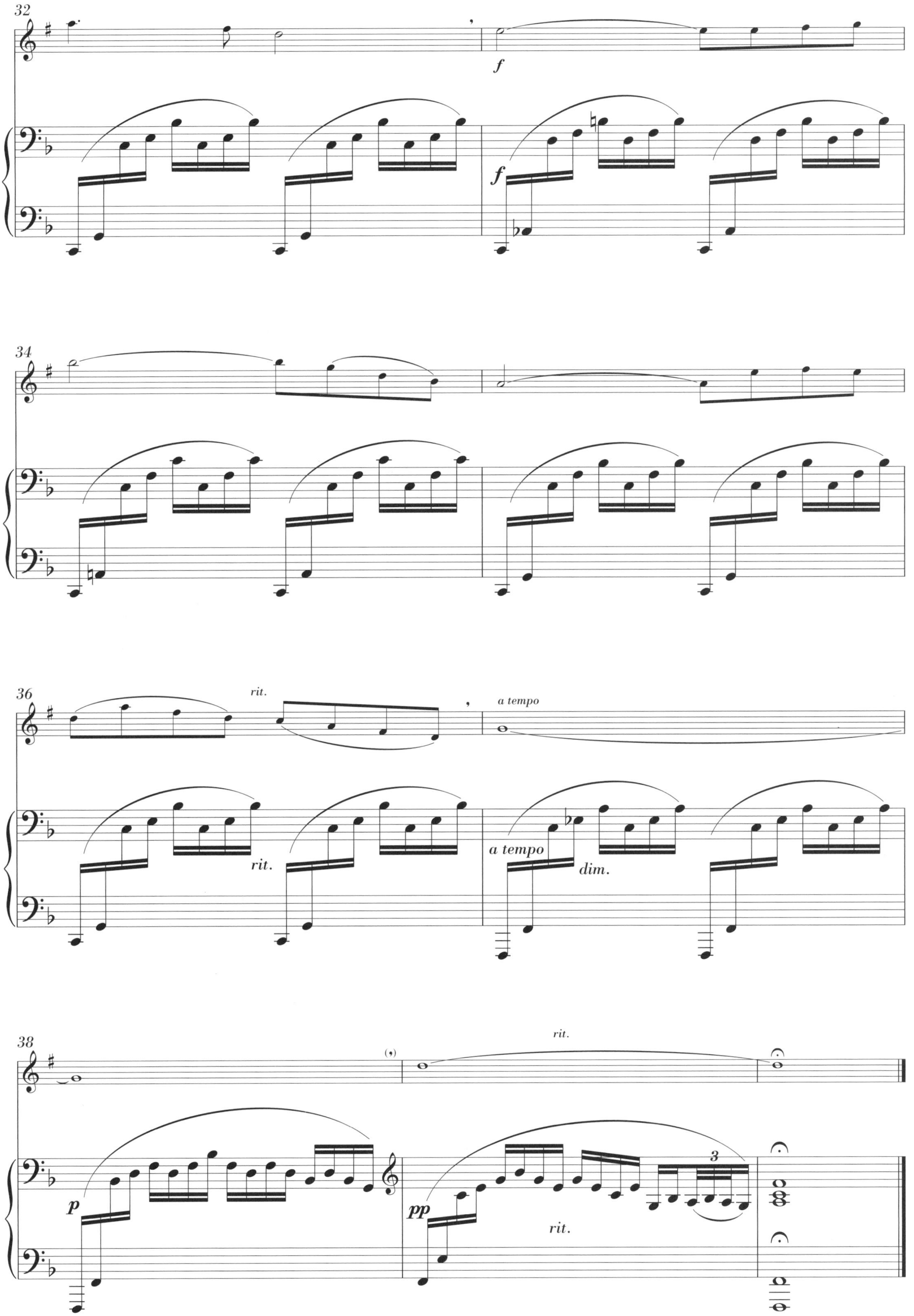
32
f
f
34
36
rit.
a tempo
rit.
a tempo
dim.
38
(,)
rit.
p
pp
3
rit.

Hornpipe

from *Water Music*, HWV 348

George Frideric Handel
Transcribed by Celeste Avery

21
25
p
pp
mf
30
mf
mp
35
f
mf
rit. last time
rit. last time
optional ending
Fine

40
a tempo
p
p a tempo
44
cresc.
cresc.
f
f
48
pp
cresc.
tr
tr
tr
pp cresc.
52
f
f
f
f
p
f
p
f

57
p cresc.
f
p cresc.
f
61
p
p
p
cresc.
p
f
p
f
p
cresc.
65
tr
f
f
f
f
70
poco rit.
tr
D.C. al Fine
poco rit.

Largo
(Ombra mai fù)
from *Serse*, HWV 40

George Frideric Handel
Transcribed by Celeste Avery

29
mp
mp
35
mf
mf
41
f
mf
mp
mp
46
poco rit.
mf
poco rit.

Jupiter Chorale

from *The Planets*

Gustav Holst
Transcribed by Celeste Avery

21
f
26
(,)
31
Broadly
poco rit.
ff
poco rit.
f
36
8va
(,)
rit.
rit.

Wedding March

from A *Midsummer Night's Dream*, Op. 61

Felix Mendelssohn
Transcribed by Celeste Avery

20
sfz
26
ff
tr
sfz
f
31
tr
optional ending
mf
p
37

43
49
cresc. poco a poco
mp
cresc. poco a poco
55
f
cresc. poco a poco
mf
cresc. poco a poco
61
ff
f
sfz
f

67
tr
sfz
73
f
79
rit.
a tempo
ff
sfz
ff a tempo
84
rit.
8ba

Rondeau

from *Suite of Symphonies* No. 1

Jean-Joseph Mouret
Transcribed by Celeste Avery

17
mp
21
f
f
tr
29
tr
optional ending
mp

33
mp
37
tr
p
41
p
46
cresc.
tr
cresc.

51
mf
mf
55
tr
60
f
f
64
tr
rit.
tr
rit.

Bridal Chorus

from *Lohengrin*

Richard Wagner
Transcribed by Celeste Avery

cresc.
mp cresc.

* For a shorter version, begin here after four measures of introduction.

Canon
(Canon in D)

Johann Pachelbel
Transcribed by Celeste Avery

Sostenuto

17
cresc.
tr
21
f
f
24
27
mp
mp

30
34
38
ff
ff
42
rit.
rit.

Trumpet Tune

Henry Purcell
Transcribed by Christopher Ruck

17
mf
mf
21
f
tr
f
25
mf
29
f
rit.
tr
f
rit.

Gymnopédie No. 1

from *Trois Gymnopédies*

Erik Satie
Transcribed by Celeste Avery

For a shorter performance, the piece may begin at measure 40.

39
pp
pp
f
49
pp
59
p
p
69
pp

Ave Maria

Franz Schubert
Transcribed by Celeste Avery

17
21
25
29

33
37
41
fp
45
pp

49
53
57
61
poco rit.
dim.
poco rit.

Bist du bei mir
(You Are with Me)

Gottfried Heinrich Stölzel
Transcribed by Celeste Avery

16
cresc.
cresc.
20
p
p
24
pp cresc.
f
pp cresc.
f
28
mf
mf

32
p cresc.
p cresc.
36
f
f
mp
40
tr
p cresc.
p cresc.
44
f
rit.
f rit.